A CONVERSATION
WITH
RUTH PITTER

A
Conversation
with
Ruth Pitter

at
Long Crendon:
Autumn, 1985 and 1987

With best wishes,
Thomas McKean

Thomas McKean

Happen*Stance*

Conversation, Foreword and Afterword © Thomas McKean,
2010
Cover woodcut © Alan Dixon, 2010
Poems quoted © Estate of Ruth Pitter

ISBN 978-1-905939-26-8

Acknowledgements:
Thanks to Mark Pitter for permission to quote Ruth Pitter's
poems as part of this conversation. and for his support of this
project.

Ruth Pitter's *Collected Poems* are published by the Enitharmon
Press.

Printed by The Dolphin Press
www.dolphinpress.co.uk

Published by Happen*Stance*
21 Hatton Green, Glenrothes,
Fife KY7 4SD
www.happenstancepress.com

Orders
Further copies available for £5.00 (including UK p&p).
Please make cheques payable to HappenStance
or order through PayPal on the website.
Further information: nell@happenstancepress.com

Foreword: Her American Admirer

"AH, MY AMERICAN admirer," said the voice on the other end of the telephone. I was standing in one of those old-fashioned red phone booths in London, a pile of ten pence coins at the ready.

"It's as broad as it's wide," she continued a moment later.

I had just asked when a good time to visit might be. So things being as broad as they were wide, we settled on the following day. She was eighty-six, lived alone in a small village a ways outside London, and evidently had few guests. One of England's finest poets, she was the first woman to receive the Queen's Gold Medal for Poetry, a close friend of C.S. Lewis, and used to date George Orwell—and now I was going to visit her.

Her name was Ruth Pitter. I had come across her work in anthologies, then chanced upon an early volume, *A Mad Lady's Garland*, in a used bookstore in New York where I live. Every so often another Pitter book would surface and my collection grew, along with my admiration and interest. It was the latter that enticed me to check out her entry in a dusty *Who's Who in England* (found in another used book store—I still remember the moment). Apparently more trusting than their American cousins, many entries included home addresses, Pitter's among them. Like most stereotypical writers, I had a pencil in my pocket. No paper, though, so I scribbled the precious information on the back of a receipt: *Ruth Pitter, 'The Hawthorns', Long Crendon nr. Aylesbury, Bucks*. I was going to England in a few weeks' time, so I dashed off a fervent letter of admiration, inquiring if I might visit when I was there.

Not long after, a small envelope appeared, politely addressed to *Thomas McKean Esq*. In her reply, she'd included a phone number and instructions to her house; ". . . getting here by public transport is somewhat complicated," she warned, not incorrectly. But I took the correct train, found the proper bus, hitched the final twenty miles, wandered at last into the village of Long Crendon and located her house, "the old-fashioned one on the right, standing a bit back", just as she had told me.

I pushed open the old wooden gate, moss-invaded as all old gates should be, walked up the flagstone path, and knocked on the door. She was a good height, grey hair held back with a small barrette, exquisitely blue eyes, surprisingly unwrinkled skin, an expectant expression on her face. She was wearing an old blue bathrobe and slippers, a handkerchief knotted around her neck.

Her voice was bewitching, beautiful, clear; it was rich in humour and sadness, an echo from a vanished era. Her smile came from the heart and could be both reflective and girlish. Conversation started before I'd even crossed the threshold and was still galloping along hours later.

Sometimes we sat on a faded sofa beneath a painting of a railroad station by her brother Geoffrey. There, in the dying autumn light, she recited the 'Lyke-Wake Dirge'. Other times we parked ourselves at her kitchen table, a simple wooden one, and drank tea and ate bread and cheese. And when the October sun deigned to shine, we'd stroll around her garden. There she recited these lines:

> You shall have all that grows on ground,
> There is no good you shall not gain,
> If the heart is faithful found,
> Paying in toil and pain.

I visited Ruth many times over three different trips to England (in 1983, 1985, and 1987). The macular degeneration, which ultimately left her blind, had not started in 1983 but grew more debilitating in subsequent visits. I didn't know initially that she had the reputation, in Long Crendon at least, of being reclusive and perhaps melancholic. My visits gave little indication of this: our interactions were warm, personal, humorous. I never felt less than warmly welcomed. Our friendship was instantaneous, continuing in visits, letters, and phone-calls until her death in 1992.

One of the first things she told me, seated in her front parlour below a painting by A.E.[1] and a lovely sketch by Joan Hassall, was how, when she was girl back at the turn of the last century, if a neighbour's party was felt to be lacking, she was summoned to liven it up with her chatter. "But first," she said, "Mother would check to see if my undergarments were quite clean, as I was apt to turn a cartwheel between stories."

Her "chatter" did indeed liven things up—as readers of this conversation with Ruth Pitter will see for themselves.

Thomas McKean

---

[1] The Irish poet and painter, George William Russell

A Conversation
with
Ruth Pitter

RUTH PITTER: I wonder how my work will pan out in a hundred years time. . . . You know, my earliest little piece was a love story: there's this little boy, this little girl, very fond of each other, so they decided to get married. But they said you have to wash before you're married—but all they could find was a good big puddle, so they washed in that! It's certainly a love story. I think the last poem I collected in a book was called 'So Good of Their Kind'—

> Not snakes, huge slugs. They hung
> Twined in sevenfold embrace, by a tough slime;
> Strong slime that held them wrung
> Together, swinging and strung
> In the great double helix of our time. . . .

Do you remember? The great slugs mating—who would have thought it? You know, that pair of slugs, I think they stayed together for their lifetime!

THOMAS McKEAN: Well, after being immortalised by you they would!

RP: It was a very droughty year; I found those two together, in the corner of a box, with a little pinch of garden manure left. So I sprinkled them with water and wished them well. The literature on slugs mating must be very small! But you know, I really thought those two slugs loved one another. It would seem so. But where does love get to? It gets overwhelmed. We so constantly forget how imprisoned our minds are in the notion of time and space and matter—the human notions of time and space and matter. But these are restricted by our capacities. There is no doubt about it: we use the best capacities we have to try to make sense of these things, but I think the real sense, the ultimate sense, is quite different. "Then shall I know even as I am known." Well! Wonderful!

The little things that people don't notice—when I was quite young we had this cottage in the Hainault Forest. I became aware of very small forms of vegetation that people don't notice—the mosses, and even simpler forms of vegetation, the things we call liverworts. They have distinct modes of reproduction, very different from what we call flowering plants. Still I remember the little liverwort. It lived in this occasional splash from a little weir in a small brook. And this little thing—there it was in the dusk, under the bank, living its little life. Yes, and nobody noticing it.

But blind humanity has always had notions of this kind. What about the young lions; the young lions searching after their prey, who seek their meat from God? He gives even the lion its prey. So all that, you know, comes together in my mind.

TM: Can you recall your first bits of writing?

RP: My first bits were very naïve—no doubt about that. I took a long time to grow up. I'm glad of that. I didn't like it—growing up. I would have rather retained the nature of the child. But you can't, you know; it's no good.

I can remember the first time I tried to write something down—to write a bit of poetry or something. I felt the sensation of a poem coming—the feeling exactly as when you've received a smart blow on the nose. And I remember as a child feeling that. I was five years old and had seen a derelict windmill. The poor thing that was once so busy and is now such an artifact. To see a windmill all deserted and decaying—highly pathetic!

I started writing a little something: "The old mill stands with broken shaft with bulrushes all about"—not that there *were* any! I don't think I got much further with it. But it was the first time I conceived a poem—from this pathetic sight. It's the mind that drives the mill, you know—it has to be constructed, invented. They are works of art, aren't they?

I knew a water-mill, once. It was what they call an 'undershot'. One could watch it all day. The mill pond is so deep and so dark, and the water races away, so liberated, like children coming out of school. I loved that. It's odd; I now recall a poem I wrote when I was, oh, eight. Let me see . . .

> There was a cat whose name was Ella
> Who had three kittens in a cold dark cellar:
> One was tabby, one was black,
> And the third had spots along its back.
> She called the tabby one 'Pooser Mewk.'
> She called the black one 'The Iron Duke':
> Then she thought till her brain went round and round,
> And she called the remaining one 'Ezra Pound'.

I could always do stuff like that, and by the yard! Oh, it was life to us. But, oh, the early ones were downright funny—because I didn't really realise what the motive force was.

I wrote one I remember—it began:

> Go to thy dwelling—

(we used the second person singular in the days of my apprenticeship)—

> Go to thy dwelling, the oaken door
> That modestly doth front a leafy lane.
> There shall come to thee the young and poor,
> The weary of the wind and the wild rain.
> Set them about thy hearth and tender them;
> Sing to them softly with downward mien
> Of the quiet woods, who make their diadem
> With wanton blossoms twined with gracious green.
> Give them soft couches in thy chamber dim
> And visit them to mark if they do rest.
> If one still wake, then go to him
> And lay his head upon thy quiet breast.

Oh my! (*laughter*) I never collected that one—and good thing so! I must have been awfully young when I wrote it, and I'm afraid it shows!

TM: Did you think, as a girl, that your whole life would be given to poetry?

RP: I think I assumed it. We'd been carefully nurtured to learn poetry and to read it. My parents, you see, were devoted to poetry, so everything sort of came together. So important was that little cottage in the Hainault Forest— that was a great, wonderful thing to me. And that little church in the field where there'd been a road once but now there was none. We knew there must have been a road there, because there was a great wall painting they'd uncovered of Saint Christopher, the Patron Saint of Travellers. A huge one. It's a little, old, old church—my father is buried there . . . a wonderful place, reaching right back into the past.

Being in the parish, having the cottage in the parish, he was entitled to be buried there. And there used to be body-snatching! It was not very far from the London Hospital, you see, and, what's more, there was a little squat tower to this church. One day, nobody's been up there for a long time and they found a weathered and dried cadaver, in its shroud, there on the stairs. The body snatchers must have taken alarm and cleared out quickly and left it there.

TM: Can you recall the first time a poem of yours was printed?

RP: Yes. I also recall that when I was 11 [1908] and the first poem I was paid for was printed. It was in an American magazine. I was thrilled, absolutely thrilled. I went out and ran and ran in the fields, jumping over all obstacles, bushes, and so on. I was very strong.

As I ran I kept looking out for a small boy I expected to see, swinging on a gate or something like that. I kept looking in a certain direction. I was sure I would see him. I did not see anyone, but I had a feeling that there was a small boy who would be a great influence in my writing later. I am not in the least psychic, but I think perhaps I was thinking of [Lord] David Cecil—I think perhaps I was aware of him. He would have been about five, then.

TM: Your first books were financed by Hilaire Belloc; how did he come to know you?

RP: My father took a very way-out weekly paper. It was very intellectual. The theme was Guild Socialism.

TM: That's not a bad idea.

RP: It t'isn't at all! Look at the lovely guild players we still have. My father was very keen on this. He was socialist—I don't think he could help that— anyone working with the poor children my parents taught would be furious about poverty, they really would, and quite right! He took this intellectual weekly paper, *The New Age*, run by a man called Orage.

TM: What was he like? In America, at least, Orage is best recalled as being a disciple of Gurdjieff.

RP: That was a disaster—that *was* a disaster! That Gurdjieff: he was an old so-and-so! But Orage—he was a princely man. There's a poem I wrote after he died; I don't think it was ever published. Let's see . . .

> The heart that to itself suffices,
> The word of power that cures the soul,
> Heaven's love against all death's devices,
> The part united with the whole:
> If so much strong felicity I know,
> All, save my mere beginnings, here I owe.

My father sent some bits of mine up and Orage printed them. One of them was 'The Kitten's Eclogue'. It was in fond imitation of Spencer, you see:

No hope, no dread, my little grave contains.
TM: Yes, I like that! And what else: "Everybody's emblem is mud . . ."

RP: Yes! Everybody else's emblem is mud and Bogey Baby's is "O felis semper felix"! Belloc chanced on this and wanted to know more about me. He later wrote prefaces for a number of my very early books—in addition to actually financing them. He wrote to the editor of the paper, wanting to know who I was. So he came around to see me. I can recall the first time he came to see me.

TM: Were you nervous?

RP: Oh no! I'm not famous for being nervous! No, I wasn't nervous even when I went to see the Queen. Because, you see, we'd never been put down as children, never made to feel small. We were properly corrected, of course, but there used to be a process called 'putting children in their place'. Very daunting. It could be positively bruising. One should take notice of all children do, and be positive in one's responses, I think—not that I had any of my own.

TM: That reminds me of that poem of yours—'A Crownèd A'.

RP: Yes, I remember that:
> "Oh, Mrs X! It makes me wild
> To see the way they spoil that child!"
> Cries Mrs Y, as Mrs Z
> Smirks in the wake of little Ted,
> Who grandly, on expensive bike,
> And dressed (on any weekday!) like
> The child of some distinguished man,
> Some football-champ or publican,
> In all that's best of ready-made,
> Peacocks his way down the Parade.

But the point is, that when he gets to the butcher's shop, he kneels down to stroke and talk to the butcher's cat—
> He kneels before her, as he tries
> To read her enigmatic eyes;
> He lays his cheek upon her head,

Which she does not resent, from Ted;
He wipes the sawdust from her fur,
As if he really felt for her.

No, Mrs Y, the case is plain.
The child is loved, and loves again.

There's nothing more creative than love, is there? The title of that poem comes from Chaucer—he was a great poet! Do you remember the Nun Prioress? "Her smiling was full simple and coy. [. . .] / About her arms she'd bear a pair of beaders"—That's a rosary. 'Pair' doesn't mean two there: it's from 'peratoes'—a set, a set of beaders—

Gauded all with green,
And thereon hung a brooch of gold-filled sheen,
Whereon there was written a Crownèd A,
And after, *Amor Vincit Omnia*.

In the Middle Ages they rhymed the open a: omni*a*. I've known people, one or two very old teachers when I was a child, just starting school, who'd pronounce the final a, and as a rule, the open a. Fancy that!

TM: Back to Belloc—

RP: Yes! He was very good to me. I remember his coming round to see what I looked like, wearing his great cloak. He was half-French, you know, and do you know, in wartime, they actually gave me a day off from the factory to go down to Sussex and see Belloc, who was then almost on the way out?

He had a very nice place there, an old mill house—very, very pleasant. And I went down and saw him, and after a bit he did recognize me. He was a long way out but all of a sudden he said, "I remember you." I'm glad I went.

TM: He's known for being a bit difficult, isn't he?

RP: Oh dear, yes! He was obstreperous, he certainly was! And volatile. Yes—a volatile person. But that was part of the man.

TM: Tell me, what was Orage like?

RP: He was a princely man. He was about six foot one or two, an ideal height, perfectly proportioned, and had a delightful voice. The women boiled round him like crazy!

TM: Wasn't there someone named Mrs Hastings?

RP: Oh yes! Beatrice Hastings! Yes—that name cropped up the other day—she's always cropping up! Yes—Modigliani—she lived with Modigliani in Paris for a time. Oh, she was nothing much, only she was very daring, and that made a sort of notoriety. I went there once and her pearl necklace had broken; they were on the floor, picking them up. I somehow thought this very daring.

TM: What did your parents think of them?

RP: Of course they revered Orage because he was a man of intellect and a man of high principles. A wonderful man. But of course, he did live with old Beatrice for a time, but she was great nonsense, really. All exhibitionism and blather—not much real talent.

TM: Let's talk a bit about your family; you were lucky with your parents, weren't you.

RP: Yes, very lucky. They so fostered my love for poetry, as I have said. But I do recall my mother telling me that when she was expecting me (oh dear, she must have been so young!) she actually went to her doctor and told him, "I think I know how the baby got in, but I'm not quite clear on how it actually gets out." Oh dear!

Do you know that after my sister Olive and then my brother Geoffrey were born, my mother seemed to have regular falls down the stairs once or twice a year. I do sometimes wonder if she was attempting to miscarry, but I shall never know. I do recall, too, one time when I was older—perhaps fourteen—my father came home and he had been drinking. I did not like this at all. So I punched him right on the nose. I believe I quite knocked him out.

TM: I recall that poem you showed me, 'The Cottage', the one about your father, the one you never published. That, too, seemed to show a darker side.

RP: Yes, let me see. I describe Hainault Wood, then I write—

> My father of that utter loneliness
> Was part; he was a man of great desires
> Confused, frustrated: the imperfect he
> Rejected, and so had nothing in this life.
> He talked with spirits of the tenuous air,
> And far in the black wood I often saw
> His homeward lantern, and would hear him make
> Cheerful discourse to one that answered not.

So it continues . . . let me see . . .

> And I shall gather in his crops no more;
> Saving the lifelong crop of bitter weeds
> He sowed in me, that makes me hate my kind,
> But not hate him: such offspring was his fate,
> And such a father mine: a majesty
> Of darkness orders man's unhappy ways,
> And to that empire do I bow, and keep
> A steadfast silence. . . .

Then it ends:

> I am told he will not come again.
> Yet far in the dark wood I hear him make
> Cheerful discourse to one that answers not:
> The ghostly place hath but one ghost the more.

No, I am quite sure I never published that poem. Perhaps rightly so.

TM: You've said that the cottage your parents rented in the Hainault Forest was the greatest of single influences on your work. How did your parents find that cottage? Were they tramping around?

RP: Yes—and I often went for walks with my father. I used to like walking with him very much. We East Enders naturally made for the Forest, you know: Epping Forest was the great East End forest. Father liked walking, and I liked going with him. Those days, it didn't matter about children going into pubs. I don't say that he gave me beer in the pubs. There was a time we'd have a bit of bread and cheese, you know, and he'd give me shandy.

TM: He sounds as though he could be awfully jolly at times, your father. Was he fun?

RP: Yes; he was creative. Mother was creative, but rather differently.

TM: Someone must have been creative in your family—after all, all three of you children are.

RP: My sister wrote many novels, yes, and they're very pretty. She wrote under our mother's maiden name, Murrell. Yes, she was quite businesslike about it. And really some of them are quite pretty. She worked the old Forest in very well, here and there. Yes, she was a talented girl, no doubt. My brother, Geoffrey, of course, was a good painter, as you know.

But after all, a very skilled workman—it is creative. You know, two grandfathers, one was a master cabinet-maker, which is very skilled. When I went to English Electric to give the apprentices' prizes away—English Electric is a huge concern, you know—and the apprentices there were an élite. They were highly hand-picked. They all had to make an apprentice piece. I've got my grandfather's apprentice piece upstairs. It was a puzzle box—that you can only open by sliding the parts.

To go there was a wonderful experience for me: there was a demonstration concerning the electric spark. There were two great stacks of jars, with some chemical solution in them, that terminated by great spherical terminators—some polished metal—and there were means of approaching these terminals, and where the spark happens, you know exactly the length of that spark. That was quite enthralling.

Instead of a bouquet, they gave me a beautiful electric hot plate. What an adventure! I was taken into Oxford by the local village taxi, left in the time keeper's office, at the bus station, then a very sleek car pulled in—you see, we couldn't let the company driver lose his way among all the villages and things.

So this was the rendez-vous, and we got away, and after a bit, the driver said, "Madam—would you mind if I take off my uniform and cap? If I keep it on, the lorry drivers won't let me through!"

We got very matey, but when we approached the works we had to put on all our uniforms and gloves and things, you know. Oh dear, that was such fun. My brother and his wife were living not far from there, at the time. My sister-in-law was a wonderful cook. She didn't care a tinker's curse for making one's self comfortable. Their beds! I never met such awful beds! Any old thing would do! But she could get a jolly good meal inside an hour.

I've never forgotten that day. I was taken to the train, and put into a first-class carriage. As the train was in motion, along came a beautiful waiter with a lovely tray, with a beautiful pot of hot coffee and another pot of hot milk. Just the ticket!

TM: What was life like in the Forest, on Crabtree Hill, at your family's cottage?

RP: Oh yes—I remember when I was very young. I scrambled up through a very thorny thicket to look into a nest. There were little blue eggs in it. I didn't touch them. I'd quite forgotten about that.

And I recall one afternoon. It was on Crabtree Hill and I was working with my father, repairing the cottage. It was quite a warm day and we were drinking beer, when my father looked out and saw our neighbour approaching—from the fall of the land you could see a good distance. "Good Lord," I remember my father saying, "It's old Maybrook, and he'll be wanting tea."

We knew we couldn't very well offer him beer, so I volunteered to dash off to the well for some fresh water, but Father said, "No, we'll simply make tea from the water in the rain barrel"—which was quite filled with tar—we'd been tarring something, you see.

So we did this, and old Maybrook tasted the tea appreciatively and said, "Fine tea, this—I do like the taste of tar in a good tea."

TM: This makes me think of the poem in your notebook, about the cottage —'The Wood-Path'.

RP: Oh yes, I remember that one.

> The badger's earth, the birchy knoll
> I pass, and by the hollies wait;
> And only to pay beauty's toll
> I drop my bundle by the gate. . . .
>
> White shine the walls of distant farms:
> Ethereal blossom of the plum
> Foaming from all the crooked arms
> Of gnarly stocks, tells fruit to come.
>
> But I must on, where budding brier
> And leafy woodbine loop the way,

> To draw the water, light the fire,
> And make my bed while it is day.
Then, you see it ends—
> Draw to the fire, put on the log,
> The fir-cones and sweet-smelling bark;
> Make room for every cat and dog
> And shut the door upon the dark.

Here, when I would read aloud this particular poem, my father would always call out, "No—shut the door upon the cat!"

Yes, yes, there's no doubt the images of childhood are of great influence. I still remember my earliest impressions, some of them that is—my first bird's nest, as I've told you, a sunset on a bare hill.

And then, one's childhood was much longer than one's is today—and this was a great boon, a great blessing. One's sense of wonder, of delight, was with one for many years. Yes—and I was lucky, too, as you know: my parents were devoted and we had the cottage in the Forest. No place influenced me more, and nothing read since has influenced me as much, I believe, as my childhood readings—books such as *The Golden Treasury*, which my father so admired. Yes, at the source—and I am speaking of some of the older poems—one can always find nourishment. Though one must guard against too great an adherence to something like *The Golden Treasury*. But the mind of a child—wax to receive, marble to retain. Though in my case, this resulted in much immature verse initially.

Oh, how I talk! Have I told you that when I was a small child, if a neighbour's party was becoming dull, that they would always send for me to liven it up—by my talking! So I would be sent for, and off I would go—but always, before I left, my mother would make quite sure my undergarments were quite clean, because, when I was done talking, I was quite sure to turn a cartwheel or two!

TM: Were you a naughty little girl, or quite good?

RP: Mixed, I think. Our parents wouldn't stand too much nonsense, you know. Parents didn't, then. After all, I was three years old at the turn of the century. Children were kept in order, even poor people's children. If there were any complaints from the schoolmaster, the boy would get a belt from his father. Belts were no joke then—very heavy brass buckles with a great round disc that fit through a slot. Yes, we were made to be polite, no doubt about that.

Still, I used to fight a lot. At the primary school we went to there were a thousand children. It was rough. We all went home for the midday meal—there was no school dinner. So four times a day, this rampageous set of nearly a thousand children would go to and fro. And the boys used to canter along both sides of the slowly moving procession and pull on the girls' hair, if they had long hair, sometimes bringing us down flat on our backs.

Getting fed up with a particular boy I gave him a straight left on the barko, as we say, and do you know—his parents complained to my parents, and I was taken round and made to apologise! Stinking bad bit of business! But the next time I saw him I threw him and his bike into a brook! Oh dear! I think was belligerent because I was afraid; I was afraid of that enormous mob, those rude, rough boys. I think anything will turn at bay, if it can, to defend itself.

Later, when I was older, I took the train home from school, and at the same time we girls were out, so were all the boys—there was quite a troop of them. One afternoon a boy swept into our railway coach, where all the girls were neatly sitting in a row, on the seat, and threw himself into them, so they crumpled up in disarray like an accordion.

This was too much for me. I took my book-bag, which was quite heavy with all manner of books, and gave the boy a mighty swing or two. Later that day, when my father was taking the same train home, the conductor tapped him on the shoulder and said, "Your daughter has a mighty swing!"

I remember, when we first started going to school—this was, oh, around 1902—we learned a few rude words at once. I think when I was still a child I was more interested in rude words than in anything else one learned. Yes, rude words had something.

The first day I went to school—I was the eldest, you know—there were no school dinners then. This school, as I have said, was almost a thousand children: infants on the ground floor, girls on the second, boys on the top. It was a good thing the boys had their own playground, or we wouldn't have been able to come out alive!

Anyway, the very first day I went to school I came home to the midday dinner and I got hold of my little sister—she was a year and a half younger than I—squared her off in front of me, and said, "Listen."

She listened.

And I said, "*Bum*."

She shrieked with laughter. There was that in the blood which recognized this rude word as an old, old friend.

TM: I think it's also the way children can unite against grown-ups.

RP: Yes, that's quite true. They do it verbally, when they can't do it any other way. You know, you call the teacher an Old So-and-So, behind her back. That sort of thing.

TM: What was your schooling like?

RP: I stuck on at school as long as I could because it was a very good school —not that I excelled as a student. It was a Charity School. I was outside the catchment of the charity so my mother paid fees for me with money she earned. I remember I took it up to the school safe every term. Good old Mother!

But it was a hard life, with the daily train journey, not always well fed. There was a good school dinner, but we couldn't always afford it. But it was worth it—it was such a wealthy old Foundation, they could pick and choose. We had superb teachers and this was of crucial importance to me. I'll never forget when a little Latin mistress placed on my desk a book of Ovid's *Metamorphoses*. Well, there we get the legend of Persephone. The God of the Underworld comes up through a sudden split in the earth and carries off Persephone to the Underworld. And the poor Mother from that moment is searching for her everywhere. And it's most pathetic. She never ceases, day or night. When it begins to be dark, she tears down pine branches and kindles them at the flame of Aetna—and, unresting, bears them through the frosty dark.

Do you know, in Latin, 'pruneau' means frosty; that is why we call dried plums 'prunes', because they have a white bloom, like frost. Everything hinges together, really.

Oh, where should I have been without that, without those few bits of Ovid? And of course, I did later write that long piece about Persephone.

I shouldn't have got Latin at the Modern School—my sister went to a Modern School. The second language there was German. Our second language was Latin. And I am so thankful, although it was a hard life. Oh, that Ovid—a wonderful sensation to come across a thing like that and memorise it and make it one's own. Then, when you're on a train or any journey, you can call it up—what a boon!

Do you remember Elsie and Doris? They were school-fellows of mine. No, of course, you don't! Their father was a bit of a pundit in the district where our school was. He was a contractor. It meant he had many big nice strong draft horses which his children were very fond of. But he was also one of the school governors. He was in the locality, you see. These girls used to know what went on at the School Governors' Meetings. I remember, they told me once it was said I ought to be kept an eye on!

I recall we went to Wales when we were young. Our parents took us for a good summer holiday. One does wonder how they managed—

TM: They earned next to nothing, didn't they?

RP: Well, when a skilled man's wages were sixpence per hour, I suppose teachers were comparatively well-paid. Their association, London Teachers' Association, could book accommodations for holidays; they could book seats in trains, and I remember we went once on holiday—yes, I'll never forget one lack in justice! We went on a train from Liverpool Street, found our numbers, our seats, and settled down quite happily. But presently we got to this awful junction—it must have been Crewe—it was quite a large cross-country line and there was a very big young woman, very big creature, with I don't know *how* many babies and bundles, who managed to squeeze her way into the train, putting the corridors quite out.

And our natural parents turned us out—to allow this woman, with her bundles and her babies, to sit down! We thought the basic principles of justice had been outraged! We liked sitting there so comfortable, when everyone else was such a scrimmage. Oh dear!

TM: Did you protest to your mother and father?

RP: They were not the people you could protest to. Mother would say, "It's an order." We had to do whatever she said, or stop whatever she said. No, at that moment, it was R.P.—exit on wheels!

TM: I know that now you are deeply religious. Did you attend church when you were little?

RP: No, I did not. My parents, after teaching in the dirty old East End all week, with a daily train journey, were too dashed tired to go. They sent us to a Sunday school, to get us out of the way so they could have a snooze. And they said we could go to any Sunday school we wished.

We steered clear of the Roman Catholic Sunday schools—a superstitious fear of that. We went to the Wesleyan because we heard they had the best school treats! They had a great placard which depicted a glass of red wine, and a text which said, "Look not upon the wine when it is red." It is a Biblical text, I think. I thought this meant red wine was unwholesome, but white wine was perfectly sound. Oh dear!

When I learned the Lord's Prayer, I said, "Fortnightly God" for "Almighty God"!

Little children are wonderful things. You can get reactions out of them, somehow. I knew a child of about six months, playing with a paper bag—a good toy for a little one. A bag is very mysterious. First it's a hollow thing, then it's a flat thing. I talked to this little creature, and in the end she tore the bag in two and gave me half. The idea of sharing is much more advanced than giving me the whole thing. I thought it was very good. I could write a little book about it. I thought this was the most extraordinary adventure.

Did I tell you about the two children in a pram I was talking to? I always talk to little children. It was down at the Marketplace at Thame, one day, and I saw a little shabby perambulator and a little boy sitting in it, at one end of it, and the hood was up at the other end of it, and there was a girl, six or seven months old—just at the sitting-up stage.

He was leaning forward banging on the hood of the thing—first one side and then the other. I said, "Doesn't that frighten the baby?"

He said, "Oh no—she likes it." He then said to me, "When she's big enough, we'll both come and play in your garden."

I made him shake hands when I was going away, and the little six month old put out her hand—and the right hand, too.

Another day I went to the bank at Thame, and there sat a woman, waiting for something to be done, I suppose—a document for something, and there was a little girl standing by her—a little thing about three and a bit, and I walked straight up to the woman and said, "This child will be somebody. You'll see." I went then to fill out some forms or something, and I felt a little pressure: the little child had left her mother and was leaning against me. They get the message, don't they?

TM: So your parents taught in the East End—

RP: Yes, and when they taught in the East End much of the housing there was very, very old—sixteenth, seventeenth century. And the walls—full of bugs, bed-bugs: dreadful creatures! Poor old humanity!

In my parents' time, they used to give out dinner to the poor—it was a sort of centre where they could at least eat decently, I suppose. We used to speak quite calmly of the submerged tenth—ten percent of the population. Nobody knew how they existed and nobody cared very much—and in the richest country on earth, as we were then. Everyone seemed to think it was all quite natural—people brushed it aside. I think that when you do, you get used to awful things.

I can remember when there was an awful form of tuberculosis—it was quite common—called Lupus. It destroys the bone. Of course, syphilis will produce the same effect; there was plenty of that about, too. The hospitals used to give out false noses, celluloid noses which you fasten on the head with a bit of elastic.

TM: In one of your poems, 'The Father Questioned', you write, "Where did that noseless man come from. . . ?"

RP: Yes, yes—
> O father, who was the noseless man, and the child
> With angel eyes and face all covered with sores?
> What was the woman screaming? Why did they take her
> Away, and where? Had someone hurt her, father?
>
> The unemployed are marching, singing of hunger.
> Why are they hungry? The shops are full of food;
> Why can't they have it? Now they've turned into soldiers
> And must fight and die. Why must they die, dead father?
> Who says they cannot have food, and then says, 'Die'?

Yes—I can substantiate that. Father always got us handmade boots and shoes. And he used to take us to a shoemaker who'd been taught to make boots and shoes because he was congenitally so badly crippled and had to do some sedentary work. His name was Thomas. This man made very good boots and shoes for us, but it was such a poor quarter of London that one saw these drunks, and these people with eaten-away faces. And I jolly well wanted to know why they were like that. We didn't see them in our suburb.

This is another memory: oh, when we were children, there were concerts at Bethnal Green, which is a very slummy sort of place. Sir Henry Wood put them on, to raise people's tastes a bit, you know. And we were taken to them—it was a short train journey from our home. But we were out very late in the evening for the age we were. There was a woman who was absolutely drunk being helped along by two friends who were a bit drunk, but not so drunk. And she kept going along like that, sort of circling out of their grasp and coming down on the ground. And we learned a few words from her and those friends that we hadn't known before. But they stuck to her, you know—they did see her home.

TM: 'The Father Questioned' is a very powerful poem; it's also one of relatively few that are what might be called 'modern'.

RP: Yes, I think that's true. But I wanted to keep my life watertight, to avoid influences, you see. And I did not care to be bossed about; my sister and brother did call me that, you know.

TM: Did you boss about your brother and sister?

RP: I may have patronized them a bit. I remember being photographed: we were all lined up and I was standing with a very fierce and almost military air. I always fancied being a soldier!

TM: And now you're a Commander [of the British Empire]!

RP: Of course I am! Yes, that suited me. And I was pleased not to have been made a Dame—all petticoats and that sort of thing. Yes—when the news broke about my being made a Commander some neighbours stood in formation, with their children in front of them, and the children had been instructed, and they all saluted. I liked that—I liked it very much.

TM: What happened after you left school?

RP: I worked. I was twenty when I went down to the East coast—that was during the First World War. I had finished school, and we had no money to pay for further education. I never went to University, you know, and never managed to do well on scholarship exams. There was also, at that time, a large surplus of young women. We knew very well we couldn't all marry.

And, I must say, I rather liked the idea of independence.

During the World War One, I had, for a while, this little job at the War Office, but I was looking about for something else to do. I disliked office work; it tears the mind to shreds. I saw an advertisement in the *Studio Magazine*, a very nice art magazine. This couple—their name was Jennings, they lived in Sussex—advertised for someone to do some woodwork and painting. They wanted a young person. I thought I'd try it, and I did, and it worked out very well. So I learned carpentry and many other skills, besides.

TM: How did your parents feel about your going into this line of work?

RP: They let one have one's way. I'm glad I went. Besides, I had a sweetheart then, and we never seemed to come close to any conclusion with this sweethearting about all over the place, and never got any further. And besides, he was a Roman Catholic, and that's one thing I couldn't take, so I thought it would be a decisive thing to get this job at a distance and this would put an end to this rather futile sort of courtship. Then my sister went and married him.

TM: She did?

RP: She did—and turned Catholic, too! But then, as I said about her, she'd have joined the dancing dervishes rather than not get married! Oh, there's none so queer as folks.

TM: Do you think you could have pursued your poetry with as much concentration had you married?

RP: I'm quite sure I wouldn't have; yes, I'm quite sure I shouldn't. But what about Leigh Hunt? Writing for dear life, and swarming with children. But that, again, depends on the individual temperament. And, as I'm fond of saying, it would have been cruelty to animals to marry, for there was always this greater passion—poetry—in which the poor dears would have no share! I also say that every creative woman needs a wife, but a female poet may be better off without a husband. I have never been averse to labour.

TM: Speaking of work: the firm you were working for moved to London. Then what happened?

RP: Yes, that was where I met my old friend, Kathleen O'Hara. She and I worked for this firm, doing these hand-painted things that were sold to the gift trade. She—Kathleen—was one of the sort of girl who'd usually stay at home, helping their mothers do the flowers until they can get married. But she took a secretarial job in World War One, secretary to Mrs. Humphrey Ward, who was a well-known writer at the time.

But she also got up to larks of her own, and in the end she came to the Jenningses. They wanted someone to do secretarial work, I think, to keep the books and that sort of thing. And as her parents were known to them, they were quite close together, on the East coast, so that's the way I got acquainted. We could see they were going down—it wasn't efficiently run at all. In the end they would pizzle out. We were offered the remains of a business in London, a similar business, making small furniture and fancy goods: hand-painted tea trays, letter holders. The owner was getting married late in life and was moving away. She wanted to let the whole premises—two rooms, quite nice for showrooms, a huge place at the back which had been a laundry. It was quite spacious and we got to work.

But the factory inspectress came along and said, "Unless you completely redecorate these premises, within a fortnight, I shall have you out."

Well, we got the family together, and we did just that. Oh, the anxiety! People know when you're new to a business. You get all sorts of shady people homing in on you like vultures. It was rough. I lost a lot of weight before we really got going.

Then we did get going, and very well. We got a good traveller on the second try—the first one was dishonest. We used to exhibit at the Ideal Homes Exhibition, a big exhibition centre at Earl's Court.

Queen Mary, grandmother of the present Queen, used to come along, and we used to marvel at the amount of these little things she would buy. But afterwards we thought that running a large household, a great many of these things would be very suitable. We had to laugh: always before the Queen would show up, a little man, one of her entourage, would dart up and whisper, "Tradesmen's rates!"

I kept up the business for twenty-five years, while my old friend, Kathleen O'Hara, lived. Yes, I should never have had anything much without her: she wasn't brought up to worry about money. And I was—so she had the courage to take the risks.

TM: Yes—you took a large risk starting your own company.

RP: Yes, and I knew it, too.

TM: You divided the labour, didn't you? You did a lot of the carpentry and such.

RP: Yes, and we had these girls, painting. I painted myself. I also did the accounts, paid the bills. Kathleen O'Hara was the front person. We had two showrooms. If anyone came in, she dealt with them. Oh yes, and she used to paint herself. Everybody had a specialty. Some people were good at one thing, some at another. I had learned carpentry and other skills after I'd left school, as I've told you. One grandfather was actually a carpenter, so perhaps some skill was inherited.

Yes, one did work hard. Then I had a nasty accident—it was hot weather, and I was prising open a tin of old paint—you can't get it now—and it blew up and gave me a four-penny one in the eye. Oh dear!

My friend rushed me off to the nearest hospital, a very short distance away. But this happened to be a Freemason's Hospital—only for Freemasons. They told us they couldn't treat me. But the taxi-driver who was there said, "I am a Freemason," and he signed for us. If one must have misfortune, at least one can have it in a fortunate way! But that was a nasty blow, a horrid blow!

TM: Yes, and you were blindfolded for a while.

RP: Oh, yes I was, and then I had to wear dark glasses. But, as you know, it all led to the writing of 'Stormcock in Elder'.

TM: Was Kathleen O'Hara very Irish in personality?

RP: Oh yes . . . yes, her mother and father were both Irish. Her father was a doctor, he was the handsomest man in Cork. Her mother was a proper old tottletadgit—it's a word I made up. She had a large family—she was a matriarch—she really was tyrannical.

I was at the lunch table once. She sat me next to her so she could go for me when she felt like it. And the first thing I knew was she gave me a great big bolt across the hand with a tablespoon and told me I was very impolite and I wasn't talking enough! But how could I? Everybody was talking parish-pub—people I didn't know, penny-farthing things.

When we went out to stay with them, she used to come straight into the room that was allotted to us and turn out our suitcases on the bed like that, and hold up something—a petticoat perhaps—and say, "The extravagance! It's almost good enough for me! Think of unmarried girls wearing a thing like that!"

She was a specimen! She was one on her own!

TM: Did Kathleen have a hot temper, too?

RP: No, she did not—she was very well-judging. Took after her father, I suppose, who was a doctor, and of a very traditional mind. But if I began to get fond of anybody else, she always cut up rough. One time, when I told her I thought I'd fallen in love with someone, she actually fainted! Yes, she did! All the same, I don't know what I should have done if I'd never met Kathleen O'Hara!

TM: Let's talk a bit about some of the people you've known. Can we start with C.S. Lewis?

RP: Oh, Lewis! He was one of the three men of genius I have known well— the other two being Orwell and Orage. I actually sought out Lewis. You see, I heard this lecture by him on the radio, about Christianity, and set about getting to know him. I was a bohemian then—I was, yes!

It was the Second World War when Lewis began to broadcast. He really was first-class. I went and scraped acquaintance with him at once. We became great friends—at one point, when he was younger, Lewis said to a friend, 'Were I to marry, it would be to Miss Ruth Pitter.' Well!

And was he clever! Just like a naughty schoolboy! Oh, he was a brilliant thinker. I've always said he undermined one in any number of ways. If you read *The Allegory of Love* you get his attitude there. It was a great delight to have known him—very worthwhile. But that one book, *The Allegory of Love* —it's a masterly, it's a great, great thing.

I used to like catching Lewis out, because although the man was wonderful, he was not a practical hand. I am, very much, a practical hand, and I said, "How, when the children have that lovely meal with the good beavers, [in *The Lion, the Witch, and the Wardrobe*] you remember," I said, "they had fish, I think; they had potatoes, milk for the children to drink, and beer for Mr Beaver; and I think Mrs Beaver made herself a cup of tea." I wanted to know, as the Witch doesn't allow any imports, and as it's always winter and never

29

Christmas, how could they grow potatoes, a vegetable that won't stand the smallest touch of frost?

Lewis said, "Um, I must refer you to a further study of the text."

His brother said, "Nonsense, Jack, you're stumped and you know it!"

He wasn't a practical hand; he was much better than a practical hand. It was a great privilege to have known him.

I remember going to a C.S. Lewis Jamboree at Oxford a long time ago. There was one just this year and they wanted me to go: I would have been treated as a precious relic. Well, I'd made up a poem I was rather pleased with, with Lewis in it—

TM: 'Angels'—I love that one.

RP: Do you know it?
> And if you entertain one there.
> What angel haunts your mind. . . ?

Oh, Tommy, I'm glad you like that! And I asked the Master of Ceremony if I could stand up and repeat it, so I did:
> Or likelier, now we dream of space,
> Lewis's dread sublime
> Pillars of light, no limbs, no face,
> Sickening our space and time?

Our own sense of dimension all goes to blazes. A good idea, that—a very good idea.

TM: I recall reading in some book about Lewis where they quoted a letter from him to you, one in which he wrote he was refraining from sending you some of his poems because, next to yours, they'd sound like an awful brass band.

RP: He did long to be a poet, although that was not where his greatest skill lay. Well—it was only through Lewis's wartime broadcasts that I stopped being a bohemian.

TM: Do you think you really qualified as a bohemian? You were always such a hard worker.

RP: Yes, I was a hard worker. And I was never indiscriminate in my relations

—and that's the very essence of bohemian life. One sometimes got very fond of people, you know. I was in love many times, but I never found my one true love. Oh dear.

TM: You know, before I learned about how you became a Christian in the forties, I still thought your earlier work was deeply spiritual. It seemed so informed with spirituality and perception.

RP: But not specifically Christian. No. Well, you know, when you are brought up to observe Nature, you learn holiness; it's been called the holiness of the heart's affections. Yes, it's a part of me—the informing, creating spirit—there's no doubt about that. A flower isn't just a flower, a bird isn't just a bird —more shame to the people who abuse them so badly! People are beginning to wake up a bit now.

Oh, but Lewis . . . when he met his wife-to-be. That was a disaster; that *was* a disaster.

TM: Why do you think he married her?

RP: She pursued him relentlessly. Then she worked a trick; it's been done in other instances: she developed an incurable disease. This would be sure to arouse not only his pity, but his sense of duty. Yes—he married her, and her two sons. You know, her American husband deserted them, the two boys, and committed suicide. And her two boys have been living on the royalties from Lewis's books ever since. But she did this trick, of developing an incurable disease you can't argue with: she developed bone cancer. It was a wicked trick, all the same, a most unholy trick. Quite diabolical! Poor fallen humanity!

Yes, I know this sounds harsh, so I shall say no more, except to add that, later in life, Lewis came to have quite a different point of view concerning her. He had quite seen through her. This is all in the letters he wrote me. I imagine at Oxford they're prowling about already, waiting for me to die! I've willed these letters to Oxford, you see, in fact all my correspondence, and have annotated those from Lewis, but with the proviso they remain sealed until after Lewis's step-sons have died as well. There is rather a gap between the image and the reality.

After Lewis died, they asked me if I had any letters I could spare for the Bodleian Library. I had a whole drawerful! I got a great testimonial from the Bodleian Library honoring my extraordinary munificence! And I never thought that they were worth money. . . . Oh dear; I've said enough.

TM: How about Orwell then?

RP: I knew George Orwell, and very well, and from when he was a boy of about fifteen. I knew his people. I was very fond of him, but he was such a revolutionary. He kicked over the traces, as the sporting people say. No one could help him. He was so indignant over the lot of the poor people.

TM: What was he like?

RP: He was a revolutionary! He was a bit of a bounder but we knew he was kind: he was so good to our sick old cat, the little cat Murphy. Orwell would actually take her to the park so she could eat grass which he felt would cure her digestive woes. I wrote this sonnet about her; I don't think it was ever published. Let me see . . .

> Friend, now so long under the laurel sleeping,
> Or in eternal fields with many a bound
> Hunting in glee among the enamelled ground
> Or at celestially-painted insects leaping—
> How we remember thee! for in our keeping
> Perfect in kind and courtesy thou wert found,
> Lovely in look and action, sweet in sound,
> Patient in pain, even when we were weeping:
> Mirror of manners! Though above thee grow
> Grass of three seasons, still among the flowers
> Thou liest, where are lodged all buds that blow;
> Safe in my love, thy love from winds and showers
> I keep, as one to whom it is given to know
> Choice spirits, though in other forms than ours.

But I was talking about Orwell. I still recall the first time I saw him; his eyes were an exact pair—not many people's eyes are, you know. Later, I was to help him find a flat. This was when we were living in the Portobello Road. We used to go out to dine on occasion, and I still remember slipping him money under the table so he could pay for the meal—he was frightfully poor. He did so resent this, but I told him as I was older he'd just have to put up with it!

My sister always called him "your dirty beau." He wasn't well, even then —I felt he wouldn't make old bones. Once we lent him an oil stove so he'd stay at least somewhat warm. He would show me his early writings, poetry mostly, I believe—I don't remember it terribly well—though I do remember some of it was about the flowers in Kensington Gardens, crocuses I believe, and was so dreadful we used to laugh until we cried! Like a cow with a musket, he was; he couldn't even spell the rude words he used!

But he kept at it. He had the determination, the desire for truth. I also remember one time my brother had gone tramping with Orwell: they showed up at our parents' cottage all hot and dusty. My brother and Orwell went into another room to change and wash up for dinner, and my brother later reported that Orwell was gorgeous in the buff! I do think it is a pity for such an observation to be lost, don't you? I did put him in a poem, although I'm not sure it came to much. Let me try to remember . . .

> [. . .] he's an electric eel!
> Hell! wildcats and porcupines
> battling panthers and barbed wire
> ten bobsworth of squibs, high tension cables
> and no insulation either.

TM: And you knew A.E. [George William Russell].

RP: A.E.! Oh, quite well. He was fonder of me, fonder than I knew, I think. My mother and I once stayed with him in Ireland. One time I had caught a bagful of prawns and shrimp—and when I started to boil them, lightning struck. A.E. insisted that nothing should be done to death with boiling in his home! So that was that!

I remember, too, one afternoon: I was hiking with A.E., and had left him relaxing in the sun while I scaled this rather steep cliff—this, of course, was many years ago! And during the climb my trousers split—well, not my trousers because I was wearing a skirt. You get the idea.

So I had to descend backwards. Most embarrassing! I wrote this little rhyme afterwards:

> In Eire, land of barbarous wretches,
> R.P. climbs while A.E. sketches.
> He glances up, he sees a cloud:
> "Ah, come on down!" he cries aloud.
> But she cannot suppress a dimple,

To come down is not so simple.
Her treacherous scanties fell down flat
And she has crammed them in her hat.

He was very good, a very good poet. He was fonder of me than I was aware of. He was a widower with one son, and, in his last illness he was down in Brighton, in a nursing home there, and I found people were blaming me that I hadn't gone to see him. But I never knew it was all that important. It may have been to him, but I didn't realize it.

When he died they had a great jamboree. They took him over to Clonmacnoise—it's their great cemetery, isn't it, in Ireland—and what they do on these occasions is they have the corpse in a coffin, and this coffin is put again into a large plain-looking packing case, full of shavings and sawdust and things, so that nothing can move, and they sent it up to London by train. We saw it being unloaded from the train. You could see from the hotel, the station hotel, where this Jamboree was being held, this box being unloaded from the train, and they would be taking it to Ireland for burial. The Irish are very different people from ourselves. Oh dear.

TM: You knew James Stephens, too, didn't you?

RP: Yes, he was a small man. I remember him well. He lived in this lodging at some time—and ran away with the wife of his landlord—to the back room, they ran away! They lived in London.

Little Seumas and his wife, Cynthia, had this little tiny house, and that woman, Cynthia, was one of the most wonderful I ever knew at making things go further. She used to grow little lettuces in a bit of back garden, a few herbs and things; and she used to buy what when I was young was called 'a soup fowl'. It's an old hen that's laid and laid and laid and gone out to lay and in the end it'd died of old age. They used to be very good as a basis for soup.

Then she would buy some bacon trimmings, which are very much cheaper than bacon, and what with this and marrow and bits of vegetables she would make a huge pot of excellent soup. Then she'd make a huge salad—and all out of the most ingenious contrivances. She'd give quite a nice supper for, oh, a dozen people or more, in this extraordinary economical way. It's an art.

Yes, it was quite wonderful. It was always used to be thought so—elegant economy. It was thought very impious to waste things, very impious to be too luxurious. A very old cookery book my mother had—late 18th Century,

I think it was—said one must never waste food and to remember the poor. If you had a piece of salt beef boiling, remember the poor: cut a bottom crust off a large loaf and put it into the pot with the salt pieces boiling; it will attract some of the fat and be no unwelcome dish to some of those who rarely taste meat.

Yes, that's going with life, not against it. But, oh my, when I was a child, society had absolutely no safety nets—one always spoke of 'the submerged ten percent'. Yes, it was quite possible to slip altogether through the bottom and disappear, as it were, into the primeval ooze. One must always try to be grateful.

TM: I often think of a poem of yours—the one called 'For Sleep, or Death'.

RP: Yes—it begins "Cure me with quietness." Let's see . . .

> Cure me with quietness,
> Bless me with peace;
> Comfort my heaviness,
> Stay me with ease.
> Stillness in solitude
> Send down like dew;
> Mine armour of fortitude
> Piece and make new:
> That when I rise again
> I may shine bright
> As the sky after rain,
> Day after night.

And I don't mean just getting up in the morning; it means the resurrection of the body and the life everlasting.

TM: That seems to me a beautiful, beautiful poem.

RP: I am very honoured anyone should think so. There's nothing so good as a good sleep when one is naturally tired. But never mind—one can't order life to suit one's self. Like the knight in the dungeon: a kind lady came enquiring about him. "Madam," he said, "I've abided here God's will, for I may no other."

TM: Would you say being a woman poet makes a big difference?

RP: Yes, we're very rare, you know. Just think of poor old Sappho: she went and threw herself off a cape, didn't she? I once remarked we are all strange monsters! There're not many of us, and it's a good job so!

TM: Although there are quite a number of English ones. What do you think of Kathleen Raine?

RP: Oh, I knew her well. She was born in the same square mile as I myself. Like me, she started writing very early in life, but she was emotionally quite a different person from myself. That business about Gavin Maxwell—oh, this was intemperate of her. She was, perhaps, ill-advised to have published *The Lion's Mouth*. Terrible thing, romanticism gone wrong. Her best work is her early autobiography, *Farewell Happy Fields*, when she was staying with her blood relations up in the North, where her view of nature was lovely. There was a bit about seeing the cock pheasant in all his splendour—as good as it could be.

TM: I agree with something you said once about the poet not telling all about love and every anguish of private life.

RP: That's romanticism, yes; one should always put classicism first. Of course, about romanticism one is apt to get silly because very few of us are objective about our own emotional lives. We can be objective about our view of nature, things like that. . . . Yes, it's strange: Kathleen Raine and I, we were born in the same square mile and much about the same time [in Ilford; RP in 1897, Kathleen Raine in 1908], and she, like myself, liked the little tiny growing things. She had a microscope, too.

TM: How about someone like Frances Cornford?

RP: Oh, she's very good. She was a University type. She wrote, "Oh fat white woman whom nobody loves"—that's very good, that.

I also knew May Sarton. I knew her well at one time. But I think she was always what the French call 'arriviste'. She meant to get there. I remember her well.

It is odd, the people who come into one's life and then drift out of it. Then suddenly one remembers them. But, you know, I tried not to notice the work of other people, because it tended to make one rather lurch about.

I avoided the company of other poets quite deliberately—as much as I could because they confused my ideas. One can't be a critic and a creative person successfully at the same time.

For a time, before the Second World War broke out, between the two wars, I was very friendly with some poets in the South of France. Orage sent me some work which had been sent in by one of these French poets—really, it was Roman France. France is more than one country: Brittany is Celtic, then you get into the great mass of France, and down the Mediterranean is certainly Roman—all sorts of Roman relics and Roman names. So I got friendly—because it's always terrible to write a poem in a language that's not your own; very few people have ever done it, I think.

Orage sent me these poems by these Frenchmen in the South of France, and asked me to wipe their noses and put their hats on straight! I got into correspondence with these people and we went and stayed with them more than once. Let me see—I also translated:

Brambleberries, blackberries,
Grown without our pains or powers;
Brambleberries, beggar's gain,
Oh how strongly bring again
Hedgerow searchings, eager hours.

When brown Pomona after heat
Brings lovely and elusive days
The poor fruit from the past can raise
The taste of childhood, bittersweet.

That was the sense of it. It came out, I believe, in a little magazine this man produced, in Provençal. In our time, they were still speaking Provençal. Most of the people spoke it as their everyday language when we went down there.

Have you heard the saying, *La mule du pape garde son coup depuis sept ans?* Well—there was a bad little choir boy who looked like an angel—and, you know, Avignon had its own popes—and there was this darling little boy and the Pope so fond of him, and he used to send the boy out at night with a bowl of warm wine for his favourite riding mule. The boys used to drink it himself! And the mule remembered this.

And she followed the boy, you know, and when she got the chance, when they were walking in procession, she let such a kick from her hind hoof that the boy bowled along the road like a tourbillon, in a cloud of dust! That's a sort of proverb down there—*La mule du pape garde son coup depuis sept ans*—and all that stuff's very pleasant.

But then, oh, when the German occupation came along. Stinking brutes! They took all the people's transports, even what they needed to get to work, and deprived them every way they could. Oh—them 'orrible 'uns! That's three times in a century they've done it! Oh, how the people suffered!

TM: Do you think it's become easier to be a woman poet than it used to be?

RP: Oh, everybody's having a bash nowadays, aren't they. Nowadays they've got the idea they're not going to be held out of anything. But there still not very many of us, but what there are, some of them are very good. I just mentioned Frances Cornford; that brings to mind this lovely poem—I forget the title ['Graveyard in Norfolk' by Sylvia Townsend Warner]—

> Still in the countryside, among the lowly,
> Death is not out of fashion.
> Still is the churchyard, park, and promenade
> And a new-made grave a glory;
> Still on Sunday afternoons, contentedly and slowly,
> The widows, eased of their passion,
> And orphans, picnicking, with bottles of lemonade,
> Under the headstones hoary.

One's known just such a country churchyard.

TM: You know which poem of yours I love, which says a good deal about country life—'Old Sisters' Spring'?

RP: Yes!

> Framed by the apricot that Father planted
> Against the plastered wall,
> Budding to bower them as they lean enchanted
> To hear their mavis call.
> Out of their childhood bedroom window leaning
> Listening with delight.
> Their maiden life still has its morning meaning
> Though hastening to night.

And it goes on how everything round them is going to decay—the old orchard yonder is decayed, the garden is deep in weeds—

> Hundreds of houses now where they went maying

About their father's meads. . . .
Yes, they're still in their enchanted childhood. I think it's a very good poem, that.

TM: You were the first woman to receive the Queen's Gold Medal for Poetry. You've shown it to me—it's beautiful.

RP: Yes, it was designed, I believe, by Edmund Dulac. And it's useful, too, in its way: if you have a stye on your eyelid, and you smooth the gold on it, it cures the stye. Mother's wedding ring used to do as much. You know, in the Middle Ages, gold was the cure for everything. Well—of course!—since they say poverty is the root of all evil, I think in that sense gold is supposed to be a cure. Life without security can be dreadful, you know. I do say, "No gold, no Holy Ghost."

TM: And you chatted with the Queen a bit, didn't you?

RP: Oh yes—I was received. That was quite unusual: sometimes one stands in a row, and the Queen goes along and pins on the decorations. But I was received because the Poet Laureate, John Masefield, had recommended me. I took a car from the village; we almost didn't make it—something minor went wrong with the car. Yes, we almost lost the ship for a penny's worth of tar!

And yes, as you say, it was the first time a woman had been so selected. I was able to tell the Queen that her mother had, prior to the War, been one of my customers.

Then, when leaving the Palace, came a chance meeting with Dr Albert Schweitzer, whose work I so admire. I am glad to say that I had the presence of mind to curtsey. Years later, I happened to meet a friend of the doctor's, who kindly conveyed the message who the mad lady curtseying at the Palace had been and how much I admired his work.

TM: Frances Cornford, I believe, and Stevie Smith followed.

RP: Oh that Stevie Smith! By the time she came along the medal had got very small—it really had! She could wear it on a tie around her neck.

I also knew Anna Wickham slightly. Oh, she was rumptitoo old cuss! She really was! She had several sons and they lived just anyhow. They used to get in a case of tumblers, no end of booze, and have a regular jamboree at times. Poor

old thing! Don't know if she ever wrote anything worth keeping.
    I never mixed with the poets much.

TM: Did you know Eliot?

RP: Slightly. We worshipped for a time at the same church. Of course, I've often said I felt he contributed to a disaster in English poetry—by taking it away from the common man and making it the province of the few. Still, his stature is much greater than mine—but, as I always say, an English cat can look at an American king! You know, shortly after I heard I was to get the Queen's medal, I saw Eliot standing in a bus queue—and I thought, 'I must tell him'—so I went up to him and said, "Mr Eliot, I must tell you, I am to be given the Queen's Medal for Poetry," and he said, "I am very glad to hear it. You thoroughly deserve it." Wasn't that nice of him?

TM: Were there any living writers who influenced you?

RP: They must have done, unconsciously. But none of them consciously. Of course, Tennyson—he is an excellent poet. He went out of fashion very much at one time. Lots of people wouldn't agree with one, but technically he was wonderful. Do you know 'The Lady of Shalott'? I'm glad you do, because the structure and the music of it are all its own. Has it struck you—the rhyme scheme and the flow of it are magical—

> She left the web, she left the loom,
> She made three paces through the room;
> She saw the water-lily bloom,
> She saw the helmet and the plume,
>   She look'd down to Camelot.
> Out flew the web and floated wide;
> The mirror crack'd from side to side;
> 'The curse is come upon me,' cried
>   The Lady of Shalott.

That's magical! That, 'tis magical! And 'The Brook'—children love that. And 'The Lotos-Eaters', that's a beautiful one, because in that land nothing changes—

> Full-faced above the valley
> Stood the moon.
> She rose every evening,

Full, at the same time. . . .

That's a good wheeze, isn't it? Notice the epithets; Tennyson never made use of a commonplace adjective; the epithet was always exact, and indispensable. Do you know the songs in 'The Princess'?

Sweet and low, sweet and low,
Wind of the western sea. . . .

That's a lovely harmonious poem, full of enchantment, full of magic. Isn't it extraordinary that Tennyson went so much out of fashion?

TM: Perhaps that's the danger—he was so actually in fashion.

RP: Yes, yes it 'tis—then there's this reaction.

TM: You've always been outside fashion—

RP: I didn't like it—I mean I didn't like the people who made a bid to be in fashion. I came across them; I met them every now and then. I have met old Somerset Maugham—a nasty job of work! I sat by him and he said, "I suppose you expect me to buy wine?"

Everyone has suffered from esprit d'escalier—to afterwards think of things one should have said. Well, all I said was, "Yes, I should be glad of a glass of wine." Leaving out the insolence, you see, and accepting the offer. But I wish I'd told him, "Are you sure you can afford it?" He was rolling in money. You see, I was accustomed to slipping the ten-bob note into the hand of the boyfriend under the table 'cause I knew he hadn't got any!

TM: Imagine if you had slipped Maugham some money!

RP: Oh, I wish I had. Esprit d'escalier—what an awful pain it is! RP—exit on wheels! I remember now the first large function I was invited to: I must have been very green. I received a grand invitation card from the Canadian Government for a reception of some sort. In the corner it said, 'Decorations'. It meant if you had any medals or that sort of thing, you went with them on. I thought that it meant they'd spent the whole weekend, making decorations and sticking them up!

TM: You must have been rather disappointed when you arrived and there were no decorations to be seen.

RP: Yes! But it was very grand for a person of the age I was then to be asked. I believe the Governor was there.

TM: Now, if you went, you could wear your decorations!

RP: I could. I have my CBE—Commander of the British Empire—the Empire that was!

TM: What did you think of Edith Sitwell? Did you read her much?

RP: Oh not, not much. I thought she was a joke, on the whole. She had a gift, but then all the Sitwells were that crazy. And their father, Sir George, was such a brute. . . . I've been to see Edith Sitwell in my time, but 'tis so long ago. She wasn't a patch on my own Dorothy Wellesley, though. I must have spoken to you of her. She was highly pathetic, no doubt about that!

TM: Didn't you write a poem about her—

RP: Oh, I know—it's 'So I Thought She Must Have Been Forgiven'. That *was* about Dorothy Wellesley. "So, with her everlasting cape on her shoulders. . . ." That was Irish frieze—indestructible.

TM: And she walks among costly trees—

RP: Yes, she goes out—she had, oh, quite a park. She was a wealthy woman. There were wild lilies-of-the-valley in those woods. People used to come and steal them. And she would go out to see them at night; the scent was strongest then, by moonlight. It seemed so magical. Yes, I knew her well. I wrote about those lilies—

> [. . .] She comes to the pearl-shining place, where all around
> Wild valley-lilies grow out of their rocky ground:
> So intense in their presence, so sensuous yet so pure
> In poignancy, she feels she is shriven clean.
> Faithful to their own nature, they make her sure
> That what is seen brings news of the unseen:
> That her own faithlessness is taken care of
> In some high sovereign manner she is not aware of.

Oh, she was a tragic figure. Of course, she was highly gifted, but her life was in ruins. She used drugs. She used to get hold of them in all sorts of ways You know, hardcore ways—people *will* get them.

I first met her—it was during the last war; they'd given me the day off from the factory to go down to a meeting of a poetry society in Tunbridge Wells. The poetry society was invented and sort of leased-out by someone who called himself the chevalier of something-or-other. Yes, he did! It was like the hamburgers: they had branches all over the place. And all the ladies of a certain age belonged.

I was asked to go down to speak to the Tunbridge Wells branch. Dorothy Wellesley gave a supper party afterwards for all the village spins, anyone who wrote a bit—there was quite a number of them. Her dining room was done up by people who were really in the forefront of modern art décor: beastly painted furniture; curtains with great lumps of mirror sewn into them. Awful! And larger than life-size murals, huge nude figures draping around the walls. Oh dear!

After the tumult and shouting had died down, and all the village spins had gone home, she came to me and said, "I need a friend!" in the most pathetic way. And oh, she did need a friend! It was gruelling hard work to be a friend of Dorothy Wellesley. In her case, it was so genuinely pathetic, so childish. It was really a terrible thing. I don't know why her husband left her in the lurch. He wasn't a nice person, I think.

Anyhow, it was wartime, and her daughter was married and the son serving with his regiment, so she was very lonely. I used to go to and fro. Any weekend I could I used to go down to her.

But along comes C.S. Lewis. He starts broadcasting, you know. They got him doing pep talks on the air—talking to military camps, that sort of thing. I remember seeing a poor man in the train holding up the little booklets that were sold—Lewis's—and saying, "He's got it all here! Got it all here!" Like the brazen serpent in the wilderness. The man had been simply knocked for six! And I was knocked for six, too.

But that didn't suit Dorothy Wellesley. She turned against me when I went under the influence of Lewis and became a practising Christian. It divided us very much because she had seen a great deal of hypocrisy in high places; she'd seen people who pretended to be religious.

Her own father died young, and her mother's second marriage was to a man—a very eminent person—her step-father—he was Prior of the Order of the Knights of St. John of Jerusalem. Very important Christian. And he was anything but. In his private life he did just as he pleased. He himself was a corrupted, dissipated man. And she thought the hypocrisy of this situation was odious to the last degree. Seeing this, as a very young thing, she saw what whited sepulchres great people can be. And it made her mistrustful of anything that professed piety, whether they were sincere or not. This was very natural in her case. Her step-father was meant to be a very sound and punch-packing Christian and he was not.

I, too, found something of the same when I returned to the church. I thought I had only to turn back to the church and I would meet George Herbert! Of course, the parson was simply a stuffed shirt. Oh dear. But she herself, Dorothy Wellesley, had a very clear and honest mind.

TM: Yes, I've read her poems. She seems very intelligent; a lot of her poems are very near misses.

RP: That's true. She did retain something of the amateur. Oh, the poor thing. Yet she was a true poet, there's no doubt. And, of course, she was very fond of Yeats, and he of her. I recall her quoting Yeats saying, "Pitter! Pitter? That's no proper name for a poet!" Although later he was to say some awfully kind things concerning my work.

Another poet whose work I did admire was A.E. Housman. Did you ever read—no, I don't think I ever published it—a poem I wrote in memoriam to him. Let me see . . .

> You who never made friends with death, nor saw through
> > the fraud of time,
> Found no comfort in Christ, made one sorrow a symbol
> Seen everywhere, even branding the sacred forehead
> Of guiltless nature, and writing Vanity on the heavens;
> Yet with funereal delicate sound delighted
> The pensive ear, and so adorned your despair
> That the Orphean elegy is preferred to the song of rapture—
> Dear stoic, how is it with you beyond the river?

It goes on a bit. Yes, then it ends—

> Yet a remorse attends me, that life could show him
> Such a stepmother's face: that the noble-hearted
> The well-born, fitly endowed, brave mind could find her
> The implacable blind slayer of the lovely children:
> While I, the poor, laborious, frustrated,

Look up in her eyes and trust her, though she slay me.
Though I must weep, I weep upon her bosom;
Though I must die, I return to her sacred body;
She is the spouse, and I the child of the eternal.

Then there was Auden—Auden and his contemporaries, Spender, Isherwood. Auden was a lovely person. I remember sitting opposite him once at a big dinner. I forget what it was in aid of, but it must have been very grand— Churchill was there. And there was Auden. He had a bright blue dress coat with gold buttons. Oh, he was delightful, he was nice! I remember telling Auden that there's not much catch in being a female poet, and if I knew where the Arcadian promontory was, I'd go throw myself over it! Of course, I didn't really mean it.

TM: But you know, after some point, he seemed to produce poetry, not to write it.

RP: I know how you feel! Yes, yes indeed. That whole school of thought was thoroughly damned by a man—Sir George Rostrevor Hamilton—who wrote a little book called *The Telltale Article*, about the word 'the' being terribly overworked by that whole school. This gentleman who wrote the little book called it "the superior wink of the shared secret." That was clever!

TM: Yes, if one overuses the word 'the', one ends up writing lists of things.

RP: True, but if you use it well, it's very effective.

TM: And when you drop it, it strengthens the noun.

RP: Yes. It's a question of instinct, really. It's something inborn. It's not something that is acquired by study, that sort of skill.
  Then there's E. Nesbit! Oh, E. Nesbit! I thought I knew all those books by heart! Oh yes—*The Amulet*—they participated in the overwhelming of Atlantis, didn't they. What a wonderful writer she was, so very expert.

TM: You know, sometimes in books they call you a post-Georgian, whatever that is!

RP: Oh well! Let the experts get on with it, it doesn't really matter.

TM: I'd say you were beyond any label.

RP: Well, I think a genuine poet has to be. When you think of William Blake—he was in a kettle all his own. Isn't it comfortable in this room, with that fire?

TM: Yes, that fire adds a lot. Probably your old Cottage had a nice fire-place, didn't it?

RP: Oh yes! We liked that! An old-fashioned stove with a fire on one side and it heats from under—on the left, you see, and boils a kettle. And the oven had little shelves that went round so you could get a thing evenly cooked. Once you understood it, it was a very good little thing.

There was that dear little boy I was such friends with. There were three cottages on this hill, and he and his parents lived in the top cottage. He was a little, little chap about four. He used to come and help me stoutly on Saturday afternoons—in the garden, you know.

There were some blue forget-me-nots and white forget-me-nots. You put first one and then the other all along there. The child, who was young, would do that. At the end of the afternoon's work, he would say, "Now I'll change my boots and clean them; I'll clean the tools and put them away." He said, "I'll wash my face and comb my hair and I'll have my tea."

We used to take down a very nice orange cake from a lady's shop that I knew. We'd take it out, and a pot of home-made orange marmalade and a pound of fresh butter and—oh yes!—a good dried haddock. Something like that would make a most substantial dish at tea-time. And this little creature would thoroughly enjoy his tea, but what with the hard work and the good cheer and the warmth of the fire he was by now very drowsy. He'd say, "Say a word. . . ."

He meant a bit of de la Mare's—about when the gardener's finished planting his plants, the sun goes down, the moon begins to rise, the old thrush, the enemy to slugs and snails, takes himself off to roost, and the slugs and the snails come out to eat the young plants that the gardener's just planted. And this child thought it was the joke of the wide world. Let's see—it went—

"Come!" said Old Shellover.
"What?" says Creep.
"The horny old Gardener's fast asleep;

The fat cock Thrush
To his nest has gone,
And the dew shines bright
In the rising Moon;
Old Sallie Worm from her hole doth peep;
Come!" said Old Shellover.
"Ay!" said Creep.

That's delightful, isn't it? Yes, that little boy was as good a friend as anyone could wish to have.

TM: You used to grow a lot of your food here, didn't you?

RP: Oh yes—this was a nursery garden here. And there was a lot more of it, too, where those little houses are built. There was nothing built there at the time. I grubbed up some very nice things. The orchard, of course, was there, which was about half the extent, and I had to break up the ground, but we made turf stacks, which is a most valuable thing to have because you can put them down and have very lovely soil.

So I soon got going and I had lettuce, fully hearted, the beginning of April, that sort of thing. Oh, I gloried in that. We had soft fruit: we had currants, raspberries, and gooseberries and we planted some rhubarb. All that, I gloried in it very much. I hate not being able to do it now.

We didn't have too many flowers, though I always stocked these beds here in front nicely, and I always had some greenhouse flowers. Oh yes—and down there we made two little ponds which I used to sit by, on a little grass terrace. There was a bank there and a sunk lawn. I planted the bank with partly rock plants and partly nice little bulbs, fritillarias and little small irises and things. That was very nice—we used to go down and have a cup of coffee there. I was so glad I was able to make things so pleasant for my old friend, because without her I'm sure I should never have had a penny.

TM: Let's talk a bit more about your work. You know, I think if someone were to ask what is my favourite poem of yours, it might be 'The Lammastide Flower'.

RP: Oh yes—I'm glad of that!
Now that the man is in his grave,
Now that the child is dead and gone. . . .

A farmer friend of mine wrote only the other day, asking about that very poem. What he wanted to know was whether the man, whether this really represented some emotional experience of my own. Yes, he thought this must really be about someone I'd known and lost. But no, they're quite an imaginary man and child.

> Now that the man is in his grave,
> Now that the child is dead and gone,
> Now that the summer wanes, and all
> Is housed or rotting, there again
> I see the yellow toadflax wave
> And wiry harebell over stone;
> While like a weary prodigal
> Man counts the harvest of his pain.

There the autumn flowers come, you see: the yellow toadflax, kind of a wild snapdragon, a very pretty thing, and the harebell, you know, the real bluebell, not the wild hyacinth, with a beautiful blue vaulted shaped bell.

TM: That poem ends so beautifully—

RP: Let's see—

> The yellow toadflax said, "Be still.
> I see the Powers, they see me,
> I see those Two, and both are gold:
> Two golds in one, and both are true.
> I gaze, but cannot gaze my fill.
> I can but look, I can but be,
> I can but speak it as of old."
> The vaulted harebell, "In the blue."
> "Two golds," they said, and "In the blue."

TM: One thing I particularly admire in your poetry is its clarity.

RP: Yes, thank you. You know, I've said before that I feel a poem begins and ends in mystery, but that not withstanding, I do feel one must take one's meaning as far as one can. Then, should obscurity descend, one can say it's of a divine nature; it has some sort of blessing upon it.

TM: Yes, although that of course is counter to much current writing.

RP: So I imagine. But I do feel that obscurity of an intentional nature is invalid—the sort of thing where one had to be at a certain gathering, or whatever, to make sense of a poem. No, I say take your meaning as far as it can go.

TM: Do you recall the actual moment of writing some of your poems?

RP: Many pieces I can recall the shock of suddenly conceiving it. As I've told you, the inspiration to write a poem came like a sharp blow, right on the nose. I felt if I could only get a few words out, I could draw out the rest, as if on a string.

TM: Did you rewrite much?

RP: No—not much. I think they were all quite quick. It's a different part of the brain, I suppose, from other writing. Like a bird singing—it sings because it must. Yes, I like that.

TM: Did you find writing difficult?

RP: More so as time went on. The impulse of lyrical poetry does tend to die out as one gets older, and perhaps that's rightfully so. And, of course, there are poets enough without me!

TM: Are you still writing?

RP: No—the light went out.

TM: You know, some of your early poems were quite revolutionary, such as 'Cockroach': "Modern, you call yourselves modern. . ."

RP: Yes! I'd quite forgotten 'Cockroach'. That *was* rather smart, wasn't it. How did that go. . . ?
>Yes, it's a bit too thick
>The way you copy every trick.
Here, of course, it's the cockroach speaking:
>I and no one else invented
>Cannibalism, and now you

> Tear your pals in pieces too.
> I ought to have patented
> Some ideas at any rate . . .

TM: In that book, *A Mad Lady's Garland,* you had quite a number of interesting pieces.

RP: Yes—do you know 'The Coffin Worm'? That was rather smart, in its way. It was worthy of the 17th century.

TM: I like the one about the spider.

RP: Oh yes, 'The Virtuous Female Spider'. It's grand, isn't it, her being quite so sure she was going to heaven. Spiders *are* horrible things; they are, indeed. They're very intelligent—it's an asset to them, to be as repellent as all that.

I remember once, I was at the house of the David Cecils in Oxford. It was during the last War and they were living in a little tiny house and Lewis was there. And a great spider came out from under the sofa where David Cecil's wife, Lewis, and I were sitting, and of course David Cecil's wife said, "Oh! Do get rid of it, David!"

And I noticed that Lewis minded that spider—he shied away from it. He wouldn't have picked it up—I'm sure he wouldn't.

So David gently brushed it in his hand and took it away like that. One does remember and pinpoint odd things, doesn't one?

TM: About what you call your 'profane' pieces: I have to ask, Was there really a rude potato?

RP: Oh—everyone has met a rude potato in their life, though some are ruder than others. They have every kind of rudeness, they have. Yes, there was a real rude potato. That is a true story—

> O Science! Can you make us mirth
> Like this dull apple of the earth?
> And what in art can do us good
> Like this, so nourishing, so lewd?
> Only by life such joy is lent,
> Wild, bracing, and inconsequent.

That's good, isn't it?

TM: The whole book is good.

RP: Yes, I'm fond of it. And I think *Pitter On Cats* is rather nice. Poor old Plainey who got the turkey leg at long, long last. That was a real cat. And Granny-Winks, who got left behind.

TM: At Crabtree Hill, right?

RP: Yes, yes—so she was. Poor Granny-Winks. Do you know my famous piece?—oh no, I don't think I ever turned that into a poem. I tell it to people sometimes.

A wonderful dream: I dreamt I was sitting on a very beautiful, artistic marble sort of bench, in a garden full of roses on the most beautiful day you can imagine. And down the walk came a prince. He had a beautiful face. He had a golden circlet on his lovely fair hair. He had one of those collars of S's, you know—one of those old-fashioned things they had. He had a diamond star on his breast and a sword with a jewelled hilt. He came and sat down on the beautiful marble bench by my side, put his left arm around my shoulders, leaning forward he took my right hand in his and began to murmur words of love.

But oh—awful doubt! Frightful doubt! Oh—looks can be cruel! But surely not as cruel as that! But it 'tis—his breath smelled of onions! It did! And I was so distressed that I woke—and all was revealed!

It was our great fat cat, Purser O'Hara, who had been in the kitchen, and had eaten up the remains of a very oniony Irish stew, and was asleep with his head on my shoulder, purring his heart out!

TM: I've also enjoyed your poems about children.

RP: Yes, it's startling how brave children can be. And without being taught. Yes, it's very necessary after all, these mechanics of defence. One educates one's self in self-discipline, and in not giving one's self away. For when others can tell what and how you're feeling, you've lost a trick.

But poor old babies—poor defenceless little things. I've always thought things were tough! Most babies, in a way, they have to learn such a lot. You can tell by the way they cry that they're not finding it a bed of roses.

I used to wonder, when I was young, if grown-up people ever cried in the night, without making any noise, since everybody must cry at some time or another. I used to think how nice it would be if one could go about and speak to them, perhaps give them a kiss, and sit by them until they fell asleep. There must be people who are awake, tormented in their minds.

TM: Yes, I'm afraid so. You know, that brings to mind a poem of yours—about the ghost.

RP: I remember that one; I do know which you mean ['Bloweth Where It Listeth']—

> My ghost goes about while I stay here,
> Like any wandering moth it flits abroad in air;
> Seeking the unsought, and loving what is lone,
> The cloudy-minded poor, and the weed by the cold stone. . . .

Yes, that is how it begins. Then it goes on to say—

> [. . .] it goes about blessing, and will not be gainsaid,
> The wild weeds in the waste land, the ruined wall and the dead;
> And the hearts of poor women in the cold countryside
> It goes about blessing, and will not be denied.

TM: You've written many poems about old women.

RP: Yes, that's true—'An Old Woman Speaks of the Moon', 'The Old Woman', 'Old, Husbandless, Childless'—indeed I have. Here's one I don't think I published. The title ['The Disinherited'] escapes me—

> A certain kind of little Beast,
> Too gentle to be called a Brute,
> If given Bananas, makes his feast
> Upon the skin, and not the fruit.
> The larger beasts, through ages dim,
> Have taught him fruit is not for him.
>
> And calling in this year of grace
> Upon our most ancient village dame,
> I held before her withered face
> Some grapes, and bade her eat the same:
> She knew her place, she went on strike:
> "Nay! Them is more for gentry like!"

Yes, I hadn't thought of that for a long, long time. Do you know, I am now remembering another. I recall the poem ['To F.P.', 1924]—but not for whom it was written!

> She knows not how fair she is for she thinks she is old;
> The Sun has gone, and she sees not that pure round Moon
> Because the petal has fallen and earth is cold.
>
> She knows not that she is loved and thinks she is lone;
> Voices have ceased, and she hears not that song in the air
> That carries eternal beauty for burthen and undertone.

So it continues. Then, it ends like this; now it is the song in the air that is speaking—

> Her songs are crystals born of the cold of eternity,
> Having the forms of stars, and not the colours of flowers:
> Bloom, O bud of the field! I have taken her unto me.

TM: You've written very, very few love poems.

RP: Very few, yes.

TM: I particularly admire 'If You Came'.

RP: Yes, that's an early one—

> If you came to my secret glade,
>   Weary with heat,
> I would set you down in the shade,
>   I would wash your feet.
>
> If you came in the winter sad,
>   Wanting for bread,
> I would give you the last that I had,
>   I would give you my bed.

That's not to say—that's not erotic. It means giving up one's bed.

> But the place is hidden apart
>   Like the nest of a bird:
> And I will not show you my heart
>   By a look, by a word.

> The place is hidden apart
>   Like a nest by a brook,
> And I will not show you my heart
>   By a word, by a look.

TM: When you look back, do you feel proud of what you've accomplished?

RP: I don't know: God forbid I should be proud. Pride is the cardinal sin; a professed Christian shouldn't be proud.

No—I feel a satisfaction, because of the people I got to know through my work—wonderful people. To get to know David Cecil, that was a very, very fine thing; and to get to see the Queen, who is the head of our Church, among her other jobs—that was quite something.

But I would say that the brightest jewel in my crown is the consolation my work has given to those who have needed it; people one would never have known were afflicted have been consoled. You know, I was in hospital once, for a whole summer, and it was a great teaching hospital in Oxford. I was told, although I didn't see the notes on my case, they said, "Impossible to say what has been going on." One does have to reflect about the laws about our generating: each is unique, as is any mammalian creature.

I did half-wonder where I might have come from—perhaps some star. . . Perhaps a black hole—some great black hole swirling through space. You do know about black holes, don't you? I say they are more than apt to contain surprised-looking secretaries with their typewriters! I do think we give far too little thought to time, space, and matter!

TM: Or perhaps you are from some unknown tribe—like in your poem.

RP: Oh—you mean 'The Lost Tribe'. Yes . . .

> How long, how long must I regret?
> I never found my people yet;
> I go about, but cannot find
> The blood-relations of the mind.
>
> Through my little sphere I range,
> And though I wither do not change;
> Must not change a jot, lest they

Should not know me on my way.

Sometimes I think when I am dead
They will come about my bed,
For my people well do know
When to come and when to go.

I know not why I am alone,
Nor where my wandering tribe is gone,
But be they few, or be they far,
Would I were where my people are!

TM: I do like that poem! I'm also taken with an unpublished one I've read
in the notebook you showed me—'Ask a Death'.

RP: Yes, yes. I remember that one . . .
    Sick from the sneering face of hate
    You turn, but cannot turn your fate.
    The quick heart in its flesh retains
    Sneering scars and painted pains.

    On the heart they lie so thick
    That the mind is always sick,
    And would die that it might go
    From the heart that hurts it so.

    Do not die. Accept the stain,
    Read the scar, peruse the pain:
    Death comes after. You may ask
    A death when you have done your task.

You know, one comes to terms with the idea of death, as one gets older. I
shan't mind. It's part of the natural process. It's dreadful, too—for young
people naturally.

I won't mind it at all, now. In fact, I feel as though I've been out for a long
day, and I've done some useful strokes of business, done some shopping with
which one is very pleased, and now one is waiting for the last bus—and all
you can think of is to get home and get one's head down. It's precisely that
kind of a thing—get home and get one's head down.

⌐

Afterword

THE PRECEDING CONVERSATION took place at Ruth Pitter's home, 'The Haw-thorns', in Long Crendon. After she and I had established a friendship, I asked if I might tape-record her. She agreed; I then recorded most of our talks over different visits in 1985 and 1987.

Sad to say, a number of Ruth's remarks, made before I began taping her, have been lost. One was the interesting recollection of how Chiang Kai-shek came to be one of the earlier admirers of her poetry. Also gone are a number of C.S. Lewis's word-plays and jests (in Latin) that she recounted with great mirth and appreciation.

Readers might wonder about Ruth's memory. It seemed as if almost every poem she'd read since childhood had been stored in her remarkable brain (she often remarked that a child's mind is "wax to receive, marble to retain").

I, for example, had written an essay about Ruth, taking as its title a phrase from a poem she wrote in 1921, published in 1926, and never included in any of her 'Collecteds' (the phrase being "an enchantment remembered" from the poem 'North'). She gave a thoughtful look on reading the essay's title and then, almost as if from the depths, recited the poem by heart in her beautiful, resonant voice. I'm convinced she hadn't given that particular poem a thought in over half a century.

Occasionally she *did* make errors in memory; these I have silently corrected. She misquoted slightly Sylvia Townsend Warner's poem, 'Graveyard in Norfolk' (though it's impossible to know whether Warner herself had originally published the poem in the version Ruth recalled). She also reversed the two last stanzas of her poem 'If You Came' (here I admit preferring Ruth's spoken version to the printed one).

And she was partial to singing a single line from an old music hall song, whose title and other lines had escaped her memory—it went "She fell into the ice cream and grew quite cold to me".

Unusual items would surface from time to time. In her last years, she was fond of quoting the following lines, but couldn't recall their source (I've since learned they come from *A Crystal Age* by W.H. Hudson):

> There dwell the children of Coradine on the threshold of the wind-vexed wilderness, where the stupendous columns of green glass uphold the roof of the House of Coradine; the ocean's voice is in their rooms [. . .] and the white-winged bird flying from the black tempest screams aloud in their shadowy halls.

⤳